LE CORDON BLEU

HOME COLLECTION

·CASSEROLES·

PERIPLUS
EDITIONS

contents

recipe ratings ❀ *easy* ❀❀ *a little more care needed* ❀❀❀ *more care needed*

Braised beef in dill sauce

Slowly braised beef served with a creamy dill sauce makes a welcome change from the more traditional recipes for beef. Delicious served with crisp green vegetables and new potatoes.

Preparation time **25 minutes**
Total cooking time **2 hours 15 minutes**
Serves 4

2 lb. boneless tied beef roast for braising, such as
 chuck eye, round tip or round rump
I large carrot, quartered and cut into I 1/2-inch lengths
3 onions, quartered
I stalk celery, cut into I 1/2-inch lengths
I large clove garlic, quartered
2 1/2 cups brown stock (see page 62)
I small bay leaf
2 tablespoons unsalted butter
1/4 cup all-purpose flour
2/3 cup sour cream (see Chef's tips)
2–3 tablespoons chopped fresh dill weed or
 I–I 1/2 teaspoons dried dill weed

1 Preheat the oven to 350°F. On top of a stove, heat a little oil in a 2 1/2-quart flameproof casserole or Dutch oven.
2 Place the beef in the casserole and brown quickly on all sides, including the ends, then transfer to a plate. Reduce the heat, add the carrot, onions and celery and cook until golden brown, turning frequently. Add the garlic, place the meat on the vegetables and pour in the stock—it will come about halfway up the meat. Season with salt and freshly ground black pepper and add the bay leaf. Bring to a boil, reduce the heat and cover with waxed paper and the lid. Simmer on top of the stove or bake in the oven for 1 1/2 hours, turning the meat every 30 minutes. After 1 1/2 hours, check for tenderness by

piercing with a sharp knife—cook for another 15–30 minutes if necessary.
3 To make the sauce, melt the butter in a saucepan, add the flour and cook over low heat until the mixture turns from butter yellow to a pale straw color. Remove from the heat and allow the mixture to cool.
4 Lift the meat out of the casserole onto a plate and cover with the waxed paper to keep moist. Strain 2 1/2 cups of the cooking liquid into a glass measure, discard the vegetables and bay leaf and skim the fat from the surface.
5 Gradually add most of the measured liquid to the butter and flour mixture and whisk until blended and smooth. Return to the stove, heat gently until slightly thickened, then increase the heat and bring to a boil, stirring. Cook, bubbling, for about 3 minutes, or until the sauce is reduced and lightly syrupy. Stir in the sour cream and reduce for another 3 minutes, or until it lightly coats the back of a spoon. Stir in the dill, add more seasoning as necessary and cover.
6 Remove the string and slice the beef into 1/4 inch-thick slices, then drizzle over the remaining cooking liquid to keep it moist. Pour a light coating of the sauce into a clean baking dish or shallow serving dish. Place the meat in the dish and coat with the sauce. Cover and keep warm for 5 minutes before serving.

Chef's tips For a lighter sauce, use half-and-half instead of sour cream.

To prepare this dish in advance, leave the sliced meat in a little cooking liquid and press a piece of buttered waxed paper onto the surface. To serve, warm the meat in its liquid and reheat the sauce.

Baked mushroom risotto

Traditional risotto is cooked on top of the stove and needs to be stirred constantly. This baked risotto, however, needs little attention and yet retains the beautiful taste and texture of the classically made version.

Preparation time **15 minutes + 2 hours soaking**
Total cooking time **1 hour**
Serves 6

1/4 cup dried morel or porcini (cèpes) mushrooms
31/2 cups chicken stock (see page 63) or
   vegetable stock
1/4 cup unsalted butter
1 onion, finely chopped
1 clove garlic, finely chopped
21/4 cups thickly sliced button mushrooms
1 cup Arborio rice
1/3 cup dry sherry
1 sprig of fresh rosemary
3 tablespoons finely grated Parmesan
3 tablespoons coarsely grated Parmesan

1 Place the dried mushrooms in a deep bowl and pour in the boiling stock. Allow to soak for 2 hours, then strain through a fine strainer, reserving the liquid. Finely chop the mushrooms. Preheat the oven to 300°F. Place a 21/2-inch deep, 13/4-quart baking dish in the oven to warm.

2 Melt the butter in a saucepan, add the onion and garlic and cook gently for 7 minutes. Stir in the fresh mushrooms and chopped dried mushrooms. Continue to cook gently for 15 minutes. Add the rice and stir for 1 minute. Pour in the reserved mushroom liquid, leaving the last tablespoon in the bowl with any sediment. Add the sherry and season with salt and pepper. Stir in the sprig of rosemary. Increase the heat, and when bubbles begin to rise, transfer the mixture to the baking dish. Bake on the middle shelf of the oven for about 15 minutes. Stir in the finely grated Parmesan and return to the oven for another 20 minutes.

3 Stir the risotto as soon as it comes out of the oven. Discard the rosemary and season with salt and freshly ground black pepper to taste. Serve immediately, sprinkled with the remaining Parmesan.

Fish Dugléré

This dish takes its name from Adolphe Dugléré, a famous nineteenth-century French chef. The creamy white wine and tomato sauce may be served with any flatfish fillets.

Preparation time **45 minutes**
Total cooking time **55 minutes**
Serves 4

3 tablespoons unsalted butter
I small onion, finely chopped
3 tablespoons finely chopped shallots
4 flatfish fillets, such as turbot, flounder or sole,
   6–8 oz. each
3/4 cup dry white wine
6 tomatoes, peeled, seeded and chopped
1/4 cup heavy cream
1/4 cup unsalted butter, chilled and cut into cubes
I tablespoon chopped fresh parsley

1 Rub a large skillet with the butter. Sprinkle the bottom with the onion and shallots and lightly season with salt and pepper. Arrange the fish fillets on top and add the wine. Cover with a round of buttered waxed paper. Place over medium heat and bring to a simmer. Cook for about 5–10 minutes, or until the fish has whitened and flakes when light pressure is applied. Remove the waxed paper and transfer the fish with a slotted spatula to a small platter. Cover and keep warm.

2 Add the chopped tomatoes to the pan and increase the heat. Bring to a boil and cook until almost all the liquid has evaporated. Add the cream and return to a boil. Whisking constantly, gradually mix in the cubed butter. When the butter has all been incorporated, remove the pan from the heat and stir in the chopped parsley. Do not allow the sauce to boil again.

3 Drain any juices from the cooked fish into the tomato sauce. Season the sauce to taste with salt and freshly ground black pepper, then pour over the fish and serve immediately.

Chicken with mushrooms and onions

The lovely flavors of the onions, bacon and mushrooms combine perfectly with the chicken to produce this popular dish. The chicken will cook slowly in the oven, leaving you time to spend on other things.

*Preparation time **25 minutes***
*Total cooking time **1 hour 20 minutes***
Serves 4–6

12 small boiling onions
2 slices bacon, cut into 1/2-inch strips
1/3 cup unsalted butter (preferably clarified)
3-lb. chicken, cut into 8 pieces (see page 62)
1 1/4 cups quartered button mushrooms
  (leave whole if very small)
1/4 cup all-purpose flour
2 1/3 cups chicken stock (see page 63)
bouquet garni (see page 63)
chopped fresh parsley, to garnish

1 Preheat the oven to 325°F. Place the onions in a small saucepan with the bacon strips, cover with cold water and bring to a boil. Drain and rinse with cold water. Melt 1/4 cup of the butter in a 21/2-quart, deep flameproof casserole or Dutch oven on the stove. Add the chicken pieces, in batches, skin-side-down, and fry for 10 minutes, or until well browned. Remove from the pan and pat dry with paper towels.

2 Spoon off the excess fat from the casserole, leaving about 2 tablespoons, then add the bacon, onions and mushrooms. Fry for 3 minutes, or until lightly browned, then remove. Melt the remaining butter in the casserole, add the flour and stir with a wooden spoon, scraping the bottom to prevent sticking. Cook for 3 minutes, or until lightly golden. Gradually add the chicken stock and stir constantly until smooth and heated through. Do not allow to boil.

3 Return the chicken to the casserole with the bouquet garni, season with salt and pepper and place the bacon, onions and mushrooms on top. Bring just to a boil, cover and bake for 45 minutes, or until the chicken is tender and when pierced the juices are clear, not pink.

4 Transfer the chicken to a serving dish, then with a slotted spoon, lift out the bacon and vegetables and sprinkle over the chicken. Cover to keep warm and, if necessary, reduce the sauce to a syrupy consistency. Season the sauce to taste with salt and freshly ground black and pour over the chicken. Sprinkle with the parsley and serve with rice, pasta, dumplings or boiled potatoes.

Navarin of lamb

This traditional French lamb and potato stew has existed for over one hundred and eighty years and is said to have been named after one of the main ingredients, navet, *the French word for turnip. Other vegetables may also be added to the stew if desired, as in this recipe.*

Preparation time 45 minutes
Total cooking time 2 hours
Serves 4

2 lb. boneless lamb shoulder
¹/₃ cup oil
3 tablespoons unsalted butter
I large onion, finely chopped
I tablespoon tomato paste
2 large tomatoes, peeled, seeded and chopped
3 cloves garlic, chopped
I tablespoon all-purpose flour
bouquet garni (see page 63)
I cup shelled fresh peas
I large carrot, cut into 2-inch pieces
2 turnips, peeled and quartered
I2 new potatoes
I tablespoon chopped fresh parsley

1 Preheat the oven to 400°F. Trim off any excess fat from the meat and cut into 1-inch cubes. Heat the oil in a skillet and cook the lamb in batches until brown. Remove from the pan, drain off the oil, and set aside.

2 Place a 3-quart flameproof casserole or Dutch oven on top of the stove and melt the butter. Gently cook the onion for 5 minutes, without coloring. Add the tomato paste and cook over medium heat for 2 minutes. Add the tomatoes and cook for another 3 minutes. Add the garlic and mix well. Add the lamb and any juices to the mixture and sprinkle the top with flour. Without mixing in the flour, place the casserole in the oven for 5 minutes.

3 Remove the casserole from the oven and place over medium heat. Mix in the flour, then gradually add 6 cups boiling water. Mix well by scraping down the sides and bottom of the casserole. Simmer for a few minutes, skimming off the foam, then add the bouquet garni, season to taste with salt and pepper, cover and return to the oven. Bake for 1 hour. Bring a saucepan of salted water to a boil and cook the peas for 3 minutes. Drain, refresh with cold water, drain again, and set aside.

4 Remove the casserole from the oven and place over medium heat. Add the carrot, turnips and potatoes and cook for 15 minutes, then add the peas. Cook for another 10–15 minutes, or until the meat and potatoes are tender. Remove the bouquet garni and discard, then season to taste. Stir in the parsley just before serving.

Beef with shallots, crème fraîche and anchovies

These succulent steaks, topped with a creamy anchovy sauce that is laced with brandy, make an ideal quick, yet quite special, supper dish.

*Preparation time **10 minutes + 15 minutes soaking***
*Total cooking time **10 minutes***
Serves 4

6 canned anchovy fillets
1/2 cup milk
1 tablespoon oil
4 boneless steaks, about 6 oz. each
  (such as New York strip or rib-eye)
2 tablespoons unsalted butter
3 shallots, finely chopped
1 tablespoon brandy
1/2 cup crème fraîche (see Chef's tip)
1/4 cup brown stock (see page 63)

1 Place the anchovy fillets in a small bowl and cover with the milk. Allow to stand for 15 minutes, then drain. Discard the milk and finely chop the anchovies. Heat the oil in a large, heavy-bottomed skillet until it is just hazing. Add the steaks and fry for about 2 minutes on each side for medium. You may have to fry the steaks in two batches, depending on the size of the pan. Remove from the pan and keep warm.

2 Place the butter in the pan and stir until melted. Add the chopped shallots and cook, stirring, for 2–3 minutes, or until translucent. Stir in the brandy and boil for 30 seconds, then remove the pan from the heat. Add the crème fraîche, chopped anchovies, stock and a few grindings of black pepper. Stir well, then return the pan to the heat and boil the sauce for 2 minutes. Remove from the heat.

3 To serve, divide the steaks among four warm plates and pour the hot sauce over the top.

Chef's tip Crème fraîche, a matured, thickened cream, can be purchased from either gourmet or specialty food stores.

Spicy chickpea stew

*A chickpea stew with chile, sweet bell peppers and tomatoes makes a warming winter dish.
Perfect for vegetarians, these nutty-flavored chickpeas are delicious and low in fat.*

*Preparation time **20 minutes + overnight soaking***
*Total cooking time **1 hour 40 minutes***
Serves 4–6

1 1/4 cups dried chickpeas (garbanzos)
2 tablespoons olive oil
1 large onion, chopped
3 cloves garlic, crushed
1/2–1 teaspoon chopped hot red chile pepper
1 large green bell pepper, chopped
1 large red bell pepper, chopped
16 oz. can crushed plum tomatoes
1 cup vegetable stock
1/4 cup chopped fresh flat-leaf parsley

1 Place the chickpeas in a bowl and cover with plenty of cold water. Allow to stand overnight, then drain. Place the chickpeas in a large saucepan of boiling water and cook for about 1 hour, or until tender. Drain well.

2 Heat the oil in a large saucepan and cook the onion over medium heat for about 5 minutes, or until soft and light golden. Add the garlic and cook for 1 more minute.

3 Stir in the chile and bell peppers and cook, stirring occasionally, for about 5 minutes, or until the bell peppers are soft. Add the tomatoes, stock and chickpeas and bring to a boil.

4 Reduce the heat and simmer for 25 minutes, or until the chickpeas are tender and the sauce has reduced and thickened slightly. Just before serving, stir in the chopped parsley.

Venison stew

Venison is the most common large game animal and has a distinctive gamey flavor. In this recipe, the venison is slowly cooked to perfection with onions, mushrooms and garlic in red wine. It is then combined with red currant jelly and juniper berries to produce a truly memorable dish.

*Preparation time **30 minutes***
*Total cooking time **2 hours***
Serves 4

1¹/2 lb. boneless venison for braising
10–12 small boiling onions
3 tablespoons olive oil
3¹/3 cups whole button mushrooms
I clove garlic, crushed
I tablespoon all-purpose flour
I cup red wine
I tablespoon red currant jelly
6 juniper berries, crushed

1 Preheat the oven to 325°F. Cut the meat into 1 1/2-inch pieces and trim off all the fat.
2 Place the onions in a small saucepan with just enough cold water to cover them. Bring to a boil, reduce the heat, simmer for 2 minutes, then drain. Heat the oil in a 2 1/2-quart flameproof casserole or Dutch oven over high heat. When it is very hot, add the meat in batches and fry for 1–2 minutes each side, or until brown on all sides. Remove the meat from the pan and keep warm.
3 Add the onions to the casserole and toss gently in the oil until they just begin to color. Add the mushrooms and garlic and cook for about 1 minute. Sprinkle in the flour and cook, stirring, for 1 minute. Stir in the wine, 1 cup water and some salt and bring to a boil. Return the meat to the casserole, cover and place in the oven to bake for 1 1/2 hours.
4 Remove the casserole from the oven and strain off the liquid into a small saucepan. Bring to a boil and cook for 1 minute to reduce the liquid. Stir in the red currant jelly, add the juniper berries and return to a boil. Season to taste with salt and freshly ground black pepper, then pour the liquid over the stew. Return to the oven and bake for another 15 minutes to heat through. Serve the vension piping hot alongside a potato and celery root purée.

Cioppino

This superb Italian-sounding dish is said to have been created in San Francisco by Italian immigrants.
A combination of fish and seafood with tomatoes and herbs, it is delicious served with crusty bread.

Preparation time **45 minutes**
Total cooking time **35 minutes**
Serves 6–8

3 cups white wine
2 onions, finely chopped
2 bay leaves
4 sprigs of fresh thyme
2 lb. fresh mussels, scrubbed and
   beards removed
1 tablespoon fresh basil
1/3 cup olive oil
1 green bell pepper, chopped
1 stalk celery, chopped
1 carrot, chopped
4 cloves garlic, chopped
3 tablespoons tomato paste
3 x 16-oz. cans chopped tomatoes
2 x 8-oz. frozen lobster tails, thawed
1 lb. firm white fish fillets
1 lb. frozen crab claws, thawed
2 lb. large uncooked shrimp, shells on if possible
1 lb. fresh or frozen thawed scallops
4 cloves garlic, finely chopped
3 tablespoons extra virgin olive oil

1 Place the wine, half the onions, one bay leaf, two sprigs of thyme and the mussels in a large saucepan. Cover, bring to a boil and cook for 5 minutes. Remove the mussels from the saucepan with a slotted spoon and discard any that have not opened. Strain and reserve the cooking liquid.

2 Separate the leaves from the stems of basil and set aside. Make a herb bundle by tying the basil stems, remaining thyme and bay leaf together with string.

3 Heat the oil in a large saucepan and cook the remaining onion, bell pepper, celery, carrot and garlic for 3 minutes. Add the tomato paste and cook for another 2 minutes, stirring frequently. Add the tomatoes, herb bundle and mussel liquid to the saucepan and bring to a boil. Reduce the heat and simmer for 10 minutes.

4 Meanwhile, cut each lobster tail into three or four pieces. Cut the fish into bite-size pieces and crack the crab claws with a mallet. Remove the mussels from their shells. Shell and devein the shrimp, keeping the tails intact. Remove the herb bundle, then add all the seafood except the mussels to the saucepan. Simmer for 10 minutes, add the mussels and heat through.

5 To make the basil sauce, chop the reserved basil leaves and mix with the garlic and olive oil. Season the Cioppino with salt and freshly ground black pepper, stir in the basil sauce and serve with bread.

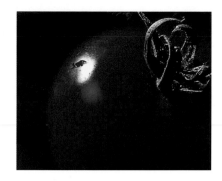

Braised rabbit with mushrooms

Rabbit meat is very lean, which makes this tasty dish even more attractive. Combined with mushrooms, shallots and tomatoes, slowly cooked in white wine and enhanced with the flavor of fresh herbs, this rabbit dish is perfect for a special occasion.

*Preparation time **25 minutes***
*Total cooking time **1 hour 20 minutes***
Serves 4

3¹/₂ lb. rabbit, cut into 8 pieces
¹/₃ cup unsalted butter
1¹/₂ cups sliced button mushrooms
2 shallots, chopped
1 cup white wine
3 large tomatoes, peeled, seeded and chopped
2 cups brown stock (see page 63)
bouquet garni (see page 63)
1–2 teaspoons chopped fresh tarragon
1 tablespoon chopped fresh chervil

1 Season the rabbit with salt and pepper and preheat the oven to 350°F. Melt half the butter in a large flameproof casserole or Dutch oven over medium heat and brown the rabbit in batches. Remove the meat from the pan and set aside. Discard the butter left in the pan, then return the pan to the heat and add the remaining butter. Add the mushrooms and cook for 3 minutes, then add the shallots and cook for 3 minutes. Add the wine and continue cooking for 3 minutes, or until almost all the liquid has evaporated.

2 Add the tomatoes and mix well. Bring to a boil, reduce the heat and simmer for 10 minutes. Add the stock and bouquet garni and return to a boil. Allow to boil for 5 minutes, skimming off any foam or fat that comes to the surface.

3 Return the rabbit to the casserole and bring to a simmer. Cover and bake for 20–25 minutes, or until the rabbit is tender. To test the meat, pierce a thick piece with a fork and lift it up. If tender, it should slide easily from the bone. Transfer the rabbit to a serving platter, cover and keep warm. Place the casserole on the stove top and remove the bouquet garni. Bring the sauce to a boil and cook for 5–10 minutes, skimming as necessary. Adjust the seasoning and check the consistency of the sauce. If the sauce is not thick enough, continue to boil for about 5 minutes, or until it is the desired consistency.

4 Stir in the chopped tarragon and chervil and pour the sauce over the rabbit. Serve immediately.

Beef à la flamande

This traditional Flemish recipe consists of tender beef and onions that have been slowly stewed in beer with a little sugar. It makes a satisfying warming dish for a cold winter's evening.

Preparation time **30 minutes**
Total cooking time **3 hours**
Serves 4

2 lb. top round steak, about 1/2-inch thick, cut into eight pieces
1/4 cup lard or oil
4 small onions, thinly sliced
1/4 cup all-purpose flour
1 tablespoon tomato paste
4 cups beer
bouquet garni (see page 63)
3 juniper berries
1 tablespoon sugar
5 cups brown stock (see page 63)

1 Preheat the oven to 350°F. Season the beef pieces with salt and pepper. Melt the lard or oil in a large flameproof casserole or Dutch oven and fry the meat, in batches, over high heat until browned, remove from the pan and set aside. Reduce the heat and add the onions to the casserole. Cook gently for about 10–15 minutes, or until soft and golden brown.

2 Add the flour and tomato paste and cook, stirring, for about 3 minutes over low heat. Gradually add the beer, then the bouquet garni, juniper berries and sugar. Increase the heat and bring to a boil, stirring. Add the stock and return to a boil, then add the beef and simmer for 5 minutes. Skim off any foam that floats to the top. Cover and bake for 11/2–2 hours.

3 To test if the beef is tender, remove a piece and cut it. If it is still a little tough, return it to the oven and bake for another 15 minutes. Once the beef is tender, remove it from the casserole, cover and set aside. Bring the sauce to a boil on top of the stove and skim off any foam. Cook for about 10 minutes or until it is thick enough to coat the back of a spoon. Season to taste with salt and pepper. Arrange the beef on a platter and cover with the sauce just before serving.

Veal kidneys sautéed in white wine

A simple and delicious dish of veal kidneys cooked with wine, shallots and herbs. The recipe may be adjusted according to personal preference by adding mustard or cream. Use these variations to transform this one recipe into three different meals.

*Preparation time **25 minutes***
*Total cooking time **25 minutes***
Serves 4

3 fresh veal kidneys, outer fat removed
¹/4 cup unsalted butter
4 shallots, finely chopped
I cup white wine
2 cups brown stock (see page 63)
I tablespoon chopped fresh parsley

1 Cut the kidneys in half and remove the central core, then cut them into bite-size pieces. Melt 3 tablespoons of the butter in a heavy-bottomed skillet over high heat and brown the kidneys in batches for 2–3 minutes— taking care not to overcook. Remove the kidneys from the pan, set aside and keep warm.

2 Reduce the heat to medium and, using the same pan, melt the remaining butter. Add the shallots and cook for 1 minute, without coloring, then add the wine and cook for about 5 minutes, or until it is almost completely evaporated. Add the stock and cook for another 8–10 minutes, or until the sauce is thick enough to coat the back of a spoon. Season to taste with salt and pepper. Add the kidneys and heat through for 1 minute without boiling. Remove from the heat, stir in the parsley and serve.

Chef's tip This is a basic recipe that can be changed to suit different tastes. A tablespoon of Dijon or coarse-grain mustard can be added to the sauce before it is seasoned. For a richer dish, some of the stock can be replaced by some cream, with or without the addition of the mustard.

White bean stew with Italian sausages

Dried white beans—full of protein, calcium and iron—are cooked with fennel-flavored Italian sausages in a creamy herb sauce, making this stew a complete meal.

Preparation time **25 minutes**
Total cooking time **1 hour 30 minutes**
Serves **4**

1³/4 cups dried white beans (such as navy or cannellini)
1 small onion, diced
1 small carrot, diced
1 small stalk celery, diced
sprig of fresh thyme
sprig of fresh rosemary
1 teaspoon black peppercorns
4 Italian sweet or hot sausages with fennel
¹/4 cup heavy cream
chopped fresh parsley, to garnish

HERB BUTTER
1 clove garlic, coarsely chopped
1 tablespoon chopped fresh parsley
1 tablespoon fresh rosemary leaves
1 tablespoon fresh thyme leaves
¹/2 cup unsalted butter, softened

1 Place the beans and vegetables in a flameproof casserole or Dutch oven with the sprigs of thyme and rosemary. Tie the peppercorns in a piece of cheesecloth and add to the dish. Cover with 1¹/2 quarts cold water. Place on the stove and bring to a boil, then reduce the heat to low and simmer for 55 minutes.

2 To make the herb butter, use a mortar and pestle or a blender to purée the garlic, parsley, rosemary, thyme and butter until smooth. Season to taste with salt and pepper and set aside.

3 Preheat the oven to 350°F. Heat a little oil in a skillet and brown the sausages. Cut diagonally into four pieces and add to the beans after they have finished simmering. Cover and bake in the oven for 30 minutes, or until the beans are tender. There should be just enough liquid left to cover the beans. If not, add some boiling water.

4 Remove the sausages and set aside. Remove the bag of peppercorns and the sprigs of herbs and discard. Mix in the herb butter and the cream and season to taste with salt and freshly ground black pepper. Transfer the beans to a serving dish, then arrange the sausages on top, sprinkle with some chopped fresh parsley and serve immediately.

Beef stew with herb biscuits

Just below the well-risen, golden brown biscuits is a rich, tender beef and mushroom stew, which is guaranteed to bring warmth to a cold winter's day.

Preparation time **30 minutes**
Total cooking time **2 hours**
Serves 4–6

3 tablespoons olive oil
1 1/2 lb. beef chuck or round steak, cut into
   1-inch cubes
2 onions, thinly sliced
1 clove garlic, crushed
1 tablespoon all-purpose flour
3/4 cup red wine
1 teaspoon tomato paste
3 1/3 cups quartered button mushrooms

HERB BISCUITS
2 cups self-rising flour
1/4 teaspoon salt
1/4 cup unsalted butter, chilled and cut up
1 tablespoon chopped fresh herbs, such as parsley,
   rosemary or thyme
1/2 cup buttermilk (see Chef's tip)
1 egg, beaten

1 Preheat the oven to 300°F. Heat the oil in a flameproof casserole or Dutch oven until it is very hot. Brown the meat in batches, taking care not to crowd the pan, for 3–4 minutes each side, then remove from the pan and set aside.

2 Add the onions to the casserole with the garlic and cook for 2 minutes. Sprinkle the flour on top and stir in with a wooden spoon, scraping the base of the pan. Cook for about 1 minute, stirring constantly, until the mixture is golden brown. Gradually stir in the wine, 3/4 cup water and the tomato paste, and season with salt and freshly ground black pepper. Continue stirring until the mixture begins to thicken, then return the meat to the pan, add the mushrooms and bring to a boil. Cover and either cook gently on the stove or bake in the oven for 1 1/2 hours.

3 Begin preparing the biscuits no more than about 10 minutes before the beef has finished cooking. Sift the flour and salt into a wide bowl, then add the butter and rub it in with a flicking action of the thumb across the tips of the fingers. When the mixture resembles fine bread crumbs, add the herbs. Stir in the buttermilk, using a round-bladed knife, until the flour has disappeared and the mixture is in large lumps, then bring together quickly into a rough ball. Place on a lightly floured surface and knead quickly until just smooth. Roll or pat out the dough with the palm of your hand to a 5/8-inch thickness, then cut out about ten circles using a 2-inch cutter.

4 Remove the stew from the oven, then increase the temperature to 400°F. Arrange the biscuits on the surface of the stew and brush the tops with the egg. Place the stew at the top of the oven, uncovered, to cook for 12 minutes, or until the biscuits have risen and turned golden brown.

Chef's tip If you don't have any buttermilk, add 1 teaspoon lemon juice to fresh milk.

Paella

A classic Spanish dish consisting of rice, saffron and olive oil, often combined with chicken, seafood, pork and chorizo, as well as garlic, onions, tomatoes and peas. The name is derived from the large two-handled dish that it is traditionally cooked and served in.

*Preparation time **30 minutes***
*Total cooking time **1 hour***
*Serves **4–6***

2 pinches of saffron threads
1/4 cup olive oil
4 small skinless, boneless chicken thighs, each cut into 2 long pieces
1 large onion, sliced
1 1/2 cups long-grain rice
3 tomatoes, peeled, seeded and coarsely chopped or 1 cup drained canned chopped plum tomatoes
2 cloves garlic, crushed
2 1/4 cups chicken stock (see page 63) or vegetable stock
10 oz. fresh mussels, scrubbed and beards removed
8 large uncooked shrimp, shells on if possible
5 oz. salmon, lingcod or haddock, cut into 1 1/4-inch pieces
1/2 cup frozen peas
3 oz. chorizo, ham or Canadian bacon, cut into 1/4 inch-thick slices
1 red bell pepper, cut into 1-inch lengths and thinly sliced
chopped fresh parsley, to garnish

1 Soak the saffron threads in 2 tablespoons hot water. Heat the oil in a wide, deep ovenproof skillet or paella pan, 12–14 inches in diameter. When it is lightly hazing, add the chicken. Cook over medium heat for about 10 minutes, turning until golden brown on all sides. Remove from the pan and set aside.

2 Reduce the heat, add the onion and cook for about 3–4 minutes, or until soft. Add the rice and cook, stirring, for 2 minutes. Add the tomatoes, garlic and stock and bring to a boil. Reduce the heat and stir in half of the chicken, mussels, shrimp and fish with all of the peas, chorizo, red bell pepper, saffron and its soaking liquid. Season well with salt and pepper.

3 Arrange the remaining seafood and meat on top and cover with waxed paper and a lid. Cook over low heat, or in a 325°F oven, for 30 minutes, or until the rice is tender and the liquid has been absorbed. Discard any unopened mussels.

4 Don't stir the Paella while it cooks because this will break up the fish and make the finished dish look messy. You may also need to add a little extra water when the liquid has been absorbed if the rice is not cooked. Sprinkle with the chopped parsley and serve.

Chef's tip If any of the mussels feel unusually heavy, throw them away as they may be full of grit.

Lancashire hot pot

A traditional regional British dish, its exceptional flavor comes from the meat cooked on the bone adding to the flavor of the stock as it cooks.

Preparation time **30 minutes**
Total cooking time **2 hours 20 minutes**
Serves 4

2 lb. lamb shoulder blade or arm chops
I tablespoon unsalted butter
5 potatoes, peeled
2 large onions, thinly sliced
2 carrots, sliced into 1/8-inch-thick rounds
1/2 teaspoon chopped fresh thyme
I bay leaf
1 1/2 cups brown stock
** (see page 63)**
1/4 cup unsalted butter, melted

1 Preheat the oven to 350°F. Brush a 3 1/2-quart baking dish with butter. Trim off the excess fat from the lamb, melt the butter in a skillet and, over high heat, quickly fry the chops until lightly browned and just sealed, but not cooked through. Remove from the pan and transfer the chops to a plate.
2 Slice the potatoes into 1/8-inch-thick rounds and cover the base of the baking dish with about a third of the slices. Season lightly with salt and pepper. Place the chops neatly on the potatoes, scatter with the onions, carrots and thyme, season lightly and add the bay leaf. Put the remaining potato slices into the dish, neatly overlapping the very top layer. Pour in enough of the stock to come up to just under the top layer by pouring the stock down one side of the dish so that the top layer is not wet. Brush well with melted butter and season lightly with salt and pepper. Cover with a lid or foil and bake on the middle shelf of the oven for 1 1/2 hours.
3 Remove the lid, then add a little more stock or water if the liquid has been taken up by the potatoes and you would like it to be more moist. Return the dish to the oven for about 45 minutes, uncovered, or until the meat is cooked and the potato top is crisp and brown. Serve hot with green vegetables of your choice.

Chef's tips Do not slice the peeled potatoes until required or they will discolor. Also, do not keep sliced potatoes in cold water, because the starch that is needed to help thicken the hot pot will be washed out.

If you wish, add one lamb's kidney, halved, trimmed of its core and cut into 1/2-inch pieces. Scatter it raw onto the lamb as it goes into the baking dish.

Braised Belgian endive

A vegetable that is wonderful braised, even though it is often thought of as being a salad ingredient.

*Preparation time **15 minutes***
*Total cooking time **1 hour 30 minutes***
Serves 4

1/4 cup unsalted butter
4 Belgian endive
2 cups chicken stock
  (see page 63) or water
I tablespoon lemon juice
1/2 teaspoon sugar
I teaspoon chopped fresh parsley

1 Preheat the oven to 350°F. Grease a small flameproof casserole with one third of the butter. Remove any blemished outer leaves from the endive and trim and core the root end. This removes some of the bitterness. Wash and place in the casserole.

2 Add the stock or water with the lemon juice to the casserole. Season lightly with salt, pepper and the sugar and bring to a boil on the stove top. Remove and cover with buttered waxed paper and then foil. Transfer to the oven and bake for about 1–11/4 hours, or until the endive are tender. Remove and place on a rack to drain, reserving the cooking liquid. Cook the liquid over high heat until syrupy. Set aside and keep warm.

3 Once the endive have cooled, lightly tie in the middle with some kitchen string. Heat the remaining butter in a nonstick skillet and brown the endive on all sides.

4 Remove the string, place the endive in a serving dish and cover with the reduced cooking liquid. Sprinkle with the parsley.

Chef's tip Before tying the endive with the string, you could wrap a slice of bacon around the middle.

Fricassee of salmon and turbot

While chicken or veal fricassees are probably the most common, fish and seafood that have been sautéed and then simmered in white wine and cream may also be referred to as fricassees, as in this case.

*Preparation time **15 minutes***
*Total cooking time **50 minutes***
Serves 4

1/3 cup unsalted butter
8 fresh or frozen and thawed sea scallops
8 large uncooked shrimp, shelled and deveined
6 oz. salmon fillet, cut into 8 pieces
6 oz. sole or turbot fillet, cut into 8 pieces
2 shallots, finely chopped
I carrot, cut into julienne strips (see Chef's tips)
I leek, white part only, cut into julienne strips
1/4 cup white wine
I cup whipping cream
3 tablespoons snipped fresh chives

1 Melt 1 tablespoon of the butter in a skillet over high heat and lightly brown the scallops. Repeat with the shrimp, salmon and sole or turbot, browning each separately in about 1 tablespoon butter. Drain on paper towels and set aside.

2 Melt the remaining butter in a large saucepan over low heat. Add the shallots and cook for 2–3 minutes without coloring, then add the carrot and leek strips. Cover and cook over low heat for about 8 minutes. Add the wine and cook for 3 minutes, or until reduced in volume by three-quarters—leaving about 1 tablespoon of liquid. Stir in the cream and cook for another 5 minutes. Gently mix in the seafood, season with salt and black pepper and simmer for 2–3 minutes. Remove from the heat and stir in the chives.

Chef's tips The salmon can be replaced with any firm-fleshed fish.

For a Mediterranean flavor, add a pinch of saffron threads soaked in a tablespoon of hot water to the sauce.

Julienne strips are even-size strips of vegetables, the size and shape of matchsticks.

Beef stroganoff

Thin strips of tenderloin, shallots and mushrooms sautéed in butter and served in a sour cream sauce.

Preparation time **20 minutes**
Total cooking time **30 minutes**
Serves **4**

1/4 cup olive oil
1 1/4 lb. beef tenderloin steak, cut into
  2- x 1/2-inch strips
2 tablespoons unsalted butter
3 large shallots, finely chopped
1 tablespoon sweet paprika
2/3 cup thinly sliced button mushrooms
2 tablespoons white wine vinegar
3 tablespoons brandy
1 cup chicken stock (see page 63)
3/4 cup sour cream
3–4 pickled gherkins, cut into julienne strips
  (see Chef's tip)
1–2 slices canned beets, cut into julienne strips

1 Heat the oil in a skillet over high heat until very hot. Add the meat and fry in batches for 3–5 minutes, stirring constantly, until lightly browned. Remove from the pan, set aside and keep warm.
2 Melt the butter in the pan, add the shallots and cook for 2 minutes or until soft but not colored. Stir in the paprika for 45 seconds, then add the mushrooms and cook over high heat until dry. Add the vinegar and cook for about 1 minute, or until the pan is nearly dry. Add the brandy, cook until the liquid is reduced to half, then add the stock and reduce to half again. Finally, add half the sour cream and return the meat to the pan to reheat. Serve with the Vegetable pilaf, dotted with the remaining sour cream and the gherkins and beets.

Chef's tip Julienne strips are even-size vegetable strips, the size and shape of matchsticks.

Vegetable pilaf

This brightly colored vegetable and rice dish makes a very good accompaniment to beef stroganoff.

Preparation time **10 minutes**
Total cooking time **30 minutes**
Serves **4–6**

1 tablespoon unsalted butter
1 onion, finely chopped
1 cup long-grain rice
2 cups chicken stock (see page 63)
1/2 carrot, peeled and finely diced
bouquet garni (see page 63)
1 zucchini, finely diced
1/3 cup frozen baby peas, thawed

1 Melt the butter in a large heavy-bottomed saucepan, add the onion and cook for 1 minute until softened. Add the rice and stir to coat in the butter. Pour in the stock and add the carrot and bouquet garni. Bring to a boil, reduce the heat to low, cover and simmer for about 20 minutes, or until the rice is tender and all the liquid has been absorbed. Remove the bouquet garni.
2 Fold the zucchini and peas into the rice. Cover and allow to stand for 3–4 minutes before serving warm with the Beef stroganoff.

Beef stroganoff (bottom left) and Vegetable pilaf

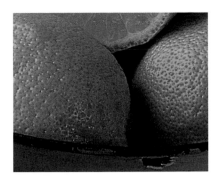

Blanquette de veau

A blanquette is a classic French "bourgeois" dish, which derives its name from blanc, *the French word for white. It is always made from white meat cooked in a white stock or water, then enriched with cream.*

Preparation time **20 minutes**
Total cooking time **2 hours 10 minutes**
Serves 4

2³/4 lb. boneless veal shoulder
I carrot, quartered
I small onion, quartered
I stalk celery, quartered
bouquet garni
  (see page 63)
I teaspoon salt
10–12 peppercorns
10–12 small boiling onions
1²/3 cups sliced button mushrooms
I teaspoon lemon juice
3 tablespoons unsalted butter
1/4 cup all-purpose flour
1 1/4 cups heavy cream

1 Remove excess fat from the veal and cut into 1¹/4-inch cubes. Place in a large heavy-bottomed saucepan with the carrot, onion, celery, bouquet garni, salt and peppercorns. Cover with about 2 cups cold water and bring to a boil on the stove top, skimming off any foam that comes to the surface. Reduce the heat and simmer for 1¹/2 hours, or until tender, skimming regularly. Add boiling water if necessary to keep the meat covered in liquid.

2 Cook the boiling onions for 10 minutes in boiling salted water, drain well and set aside. Cook the mushrooms for about 5 minutes in 2–3 tablespoons boiling salted water with the lemon juice and just under half of the butter. Drain well and set aside.

3 After 1¹/2 hours, check if the meat is cooked by piercing it with a fork—it should not resist and should slip easily from the fork. Remove the veal from the cooking liquid. Strain the liquid, discarding the solids, return to the heat and cook for 30 minutes, or until it has reduced by two-thirds of its volume, skimming off excess fat. Cool slightly. Melt the remaining butter in a large saucepan, add the flour and cook for 1 minute. Stir in the reduced liquid and cook over low heat, whisking constantly, until the sauce has thickened. Add the cream, mix until smooth and season to taste with salt and pepper.

4 Add the meat, onions and mushrooms to the pan and simmer for 5 minutes. Serve in a deep serving dish.

Cassoulet

Dried white beans are the essential ingredient in this dish from Languedoc and give the cassoulet its creaminess. Some sort of meat, depending on the region, and a gratin topping are added near the end of cooking. The word cassoulet comes from cassole, *an earthenware pot traditionally used for cooking this dish.*

Preparation time *1 hour 30 minutes + soaking overnight*
Total cooking time *4 hours 30 minutes*
Serves 4–6

1¼ cups dried white beans (such as navy or
   pea beans), soaked overnight in cold water
3 oz. fresh pork rind
3 oz. slab bacon
½ carrot
½ onion, studded with a whole clove
2 bouquet garni (see page 63)
1 clove garlic
3 tablespoons goose fat, duck fat or lard
6 oz. boneless lamb shoulder, cut into 8 pieces
7 oz. boneless pork shoulder, cut into 8 pieces
1 small onion, chopped
2 tomatoes, peeled, seeded and cubed or 1 tablespoon
   tomato paste
1 clove garlic, crushed
10 oz. fresh garlic sausage, sliced
4 small fresh Toulouse or garlic pork sausages
2 legs duck or goose confit or 1 cooked duck leg and
   thigh quarter, about 12 oz. altogether,
   cut into 2 pieces
1 cup fresh bread crumbs

1 Rinse the soaked beans and cover generously with fresh cold water in a large saucepan. Add the pork rind and slab bacon and bring to a boil. As soon as it boils, remove from the heat, strain and refresh in cold water. Cover the beans, pork rind and bacon once more with fresh water, return to the heat and add the carrot, cloved onion, 1 bouquet garni and the garlic. Simmer for about

1½ hours (do not add salt, as this will interfere with the cooking of the beans and make them tough).

2 Preheat the oven to 350°F. While the beans are simmering, melt 2 tablespoons of the goose fat, duck fat or lard in a large flameproof casserole or Dutch oven. Season the lamb shoulder and pork shoulder and brown in the casserole. Remove and set aside. In the same dish, cook the chopped onion until soft but not colored. Add the tomatoes or tomato paste, crushed garlic and the second bouquet garni. Heat until bubbling, return the meat to the casserole, cover and bake for 1 to 1½ hours, or until the meat is tender. Remove the meat from the casserole.

3 Reduce the oven temperature to 325°F. Add the sausages and confit to the casserole, bring to a simmer on the stove, then bake for 20 minutes. Transfer the confit and the sausages to a bowl and keep warm and set the sauce aside. Reduce the oven temperature to 300°F.

4 When the beans are almost cooked (they should be tender with a slight resistance), drain and add the beans' cooking liquid to the reserved sauce in the casserole. Remove and discard the vegetables and bouquet garni. Remove the slab bacon and pork rind and allow to cool. Keeping the bacon and pork separate, cut into bite-size pieces.

5 Warm a large baking dish. Cover the bottom with some of the pork rind and then cover with a layer of beans. Add the lamb shoulder, pork shoulder, sausages, confit and about 1–1½ cups of the reserved liquid. Cover with another layer of beans and top with the pieces of bacon, the remaining pork rind and liquid. Sprinkle with bread crumbs and drizzle with the remaining melted goose fat. Bake for 1 hour, or until the bread crumbs are lightly colored, then serve.

English corned beef with vegetables and dumplings

Delicious pink corned beef served with onions, carrots, turnips and light dumplings cooked in a well-flavored beef stock. The marrow may be extracted from the bone with a teaspoon and is particularly good sprinkled with a little salt.

Preparation time **20 minutes + 3 hours soaking**
Total cooking time **4 hours 30 minutes**
Serves 6

2 lb. piece of corned beef
6 x 2-inch pieces of marrowbone
bouquet garni (see page 63)
6 peppercorns
¹/2 onion
6 onions, quartered
4 large carrots, quartered
2 turnips, quartered
2 teaspoons chopped fresh parsley

DUMPLINGS
2 cups self-rising flour
pinch of salt
3 tablespoons suet, coarsely grated
¹/2 cup cold water

1 Soak the beef in cold water for at least 3 hours, remove and rinse.
2 Place the marrowbones and beef in a large saucepan or kettle, cover with water and bring to a boil slowly, skimming off the foam as necessary. Reduce the heat to a simmer. Add the bouquet garni, peppercorns and the ¹/2 onion. Partially cover the pan and simmer for 3 hours. Check regularly and skim off any fat and scum. Remove and discard the bouquet garni, peppercorns and onion. Add the quartered onions, carrots and turnips and simmer for 40 minutes.
3 Begin to prepare the dumplings 30 minutes before the beef is cooked. Sift the flour and salt into a bowl and stir in the suet. Make a well in the center, add a little water, and mix in the flour using a fork. Add enough of the water to make a soft, but not sticky dough, then knead gently until smooth. Shape, with floured hands, into about 20 dumplings. Add to the pan of beef and simmer for about 20 minutes, or until they float and have puffed up. Remove with a slotted spoon.
4 Place the beef in a large dish surrounded with vegetables from the pot, dumplings and marrowbones. Cover and keep warm. Reduce the stock for about 30 minutes, skimming as necessary, until it has a good flavor. Ladle onto the meat and sprinkle with parsley.

Chef's tip These dumplings could be made to be served with stews. Simply poach in 2¼ cups of simmering beef stock or well-salted water.

Steak au poivre

A simple method for a traditional French pepper steak with quite controversial origins. At least four chefs claimed to have invented this dish at various times between 1905 and 1930!

Preparation time **10 minutes**
Total cooking time **30 minutes**
Serves **4**

4 x 5–6 oz. filet mignon or rib-eye steaks
1/3 cup clarified butter or oil (see Chef's tip)
31/4 cups brown stock (see page 63)
2 shallots, finely chopped
2 tablespoons crushed black peppercorns
3 tablespoons white wine
1/4 cup brandy
small sprigs of fresh parsley, to garnish

1 Season the steaks with salt. In a shallow skillet big enough to fit the four steaks, heat the clarified butter or oil until hazing. Add the steaks and brown for about 3–4 minutes on each side for medium rare, and a little longer for medium. Remove from the pan, cover with aluminum foil to keep warm and set aside. For well-done steak, brown on each side for 3 minutes, then transfer to a baking dish and bake in a 400°F oven for 8–10 minutes. Remove from the oven and cover with aluminum foil.

2 Add the stock to a medium saucepan and reduce down to about 1½ cups. Add the shallots to the skillet and lightly color for 3–4 minutes before adding the peppercorns. Add the wine and half the brandy, stir with a wooden spoon to scrape the sticky meat juices from the base of the pan, mix them in and bubble for 1 minute until syrupy. Stir in the reduced stock and bring to a boil. Cook the sauce for 7 minutes, or until syrupy, then add the remaining brandy.

3 Return the steaks to the sauce in the pan and reheat for 3–4 minutes, without allowing the sauce to boil. Serve on individual warm plates or on one large plate. Garnish with parsley and serve with some French fries or roasted potatoes.

Chef's tip Clarified butter is used because it will cook at a higher temperature than normal butter without burning. You will need about 3/4 cup butter to yield 1/3 cup clarified butter. Melt the butter over low heat in a small, heavy-bottomed saucepan, without stirring or shaking the pan. Skim the foam from the surface, then carefully pour the clear butter into a container, leaving the white sediment in the pan. Cover and refrigerate until needed. Will keep for up to 4 weeks.

Seafood stew

There is no substitute for fresh, good-quality ingredients, simply prepared as in this mouthwatering fish stew. These scallops, shrimp and mushrooms cooked in white wine and cream are delicious served with crusty bread and a green salad.

*Preparation time **20 minutes***
*Total cooking time **25 minutes***
Serves 4

16 fresh or frozen and thawed sea scallops
16 large uncooked shrimp
1 large shallot, chopped
1 cup white wine
sprig of fresh thyme
1 small bay leaf
1²/3 cups sliced button mushrooms
1 cup heavy cream
1 tablespoon chopped fresh parsley

1 Trim away any dark veins from the scallops and shell and devein the shrimp, leaving the tails intact. Place the chopped shallot, white wine, thyme and bay leaf in a large saucepan with a tight-fitting lid. Bring to a boil and cook for 5 minutes. Add the scallops, shrimp and mushrooms. Reduce the heat and simmer, covered, for 5–8 minutes, or until the scallops and shrimp are cooked (they should be firm but not hard). Remove the scallops and shrimp with a slotted spoon and keep warm.

2 Increase the heat to high and boil the cooking liquid for 5 minutes. Stir in the cream and cook for another 5 minutes. Season to taste with salt and pepper. Return the seafood to the sauce and stir for 1 minute to heat through. Stir in the parsley and serve.

Veal chops grand-mère

Grand-mère, "grandmother" in French, refers to the garnish of glazed onions, fried bacon, mushrooms and small potato balls that melt in the mouth, making this dish a nourishing and succulent meal.

*Preparation time **30 minutes***
*Total cooking time **1 hour 15 minutes***
Serves 4

1/3 cup oil
2 tablespoons unsalted butter
4 veal chops, about 6 oz. each
8-oz. piece Canadian bacon, finely diced
25 button mushrooms
20–24 small boiling onions
I teaspoon sugar
5 potatoes
2 tablespoons white wine
1/3 cup brown stock (see page 63)

1 Preheat the oven to 325°F. In a large heavy skillet, heat 1 tablespoon of the oil, then add the butter. Cook the chops for 2–3 minutes each side, or until well browned. Remove from the pan, arrange in a baking dish and set aside. Cook the bacon in a skillet until browned, and add to the chops. Cook the mushrooms in the skillet, stirring occasionally, for about 2 minutes and scatter over the chops. Add the onions to the skillet with the sugar and cook, stirring occasionally, until light golden. Add to the chops.

2 Peel the potatoes and scoop out small balls with a melon baller. Heat the remaining oil in a separate skillet and cook the potatoes until golden brown, then drain on paper towels.

3 Pour the wine into the first skillet and stir well, scraping the bottom of the pan until the pan juices have dissolved. Cook until the wine has reduced by three-quarters. Add the stock and 1/3 cup water, bring to a boil and cook until reduced by half.

4 Pour the liquid over the meat and vegetables in the baking dish and toss to coat in the liquid. Season with salt and freshly ground black pepper. Cover and bake for about 30–40 minutes, or until the chops are tender and cooked through. Serve immediately.

Beef curry

Dark brown pieces of beef simmering in aromatic spices will fill you with anticipation long before the sauce has reached its required rich brown appearance. Serve with basmati rice, refreshing cucumbers in yogurt and mango chutney.

Preparation time **20 minutes**
Total cooking time **2 hours**
Serves 4

1 1/2 lb. beef round or chuck steak
3 tablespoons ghee or oil
1 large onion, thinly sliced
1 clove garlic, crushed
2 fresh green chiles, seeded and sliced
1/4 teaspoon ground cloves
1 1/2 teaspoons ground coriander
1 teaspoon ground turmeric
1 teaspoon garam masala
1/2 teaspoon cayenne pepper
1 1/2 teaspoons ground cumin
1 teaspoon salt
1 1/2 cups brown stock (see page 63)
2 large tomatoes, peeled and finely chopped
2/3 cup unsweetened coconut milk
4 cups firmly packed young spinach leaves
1/3 cup plain yogurt, stirred to a smooth consistency

1   Remove any fat or sinew from the beef and cut into 1/8-inch cubes. Heat the ghee or oil in a flameproof casserole or Dutch oven over high heat. Add the beef and fry in batches for about 3 minutes, or until brown. Remove the beef and set aside. Add the onion and garlic to the casserole and cook for 2–3 minutes, or until soft. Reduce the heat, stir in the chiles, cloves, coriander, turmeric, garam masala, cayenne pepper, cumin and salt. Cook for about 2 minutes, stirring constantly. Add a few tablespoons of the stock at the end if it looks as if it may scorch and burn.

2   Stir in the chopped tomatoes and return the beef to the casserole. Add the stock to just below the level of the meat and bring to a boil. Cover and cook over low heat on the stove or in a 325°F oven for 1 hour 20 minutes. Add a little more stock if the curry becomes too dry. Check that the meat is tender and cook for another 15–20 minutes if necessary. Add the coconut milk and spinach and cook for 10 minutes. Adjust the seasoning to taste.

3   Just before serving, stir the yogurt into the curry to taste. Serve hot over basmati rice.

Chef's tip When browning the meat, make sure that there is only one layer of meat in the casserole and that the heat is high, otherwise the juices will run out of the meat and it will stew rather than brown.

Chicken with tarragon and tomatoes

*This recipe comes from Lyon, France's third largest city and its gastronomic capital,
situated close to the Burgundy vineyards.*

*Preparation time **20 minutes***
*Total cooking time **45 minutes***
Serves 4

1 chicken, about 2¹/₂ lb.
oil or butter, for cooking
³/₄ cup tarragon vinegar (see Chef's tip)
6 tomatoes
1 tablespoon unsalted butter, softened
2 tablespoons all-purpose flour
sprig of fresh tarragon, to garnish

1 Cut the chicken into four or eight pieces, following
the method in the Chef's techniques on page 62, and
season with salt and pepper. Heat a little oil or butter in
a skillet and brown the chicken on all sides, skin-side-
down first. Do not crowd the pan so, if necessary, brown
the chicken in batches. Remove the chicken and pour
off any excess oil from the pan.
2 Return all the chicken to the skillet and add half of
the tarragon vinegar. Cover and simmer for 10 minutes.

Turn the chicken pieces over, cover and cook for another
10 minutes, or until the juices run clear when pierced
with a fork. Remove the chicken from the pan. Cover
the pan and keep the pan juices warm.
3 Score a cross in the base of each tomato, then plunge
into boiling water for 10 seconds. Rinse with cold water
and peel the skin away from the cross. Cut in half,
remove the seeds, then cut into eighths. Put the
remaining vinegar in a small saucepan and boil for
4 minutes. Mix together the softened butter and flour,
whisk into the reduced vinegar and then whisk this into
the pan juices. Return the chicken to the skillet, add the
tomatoes and simmer for 10 minutes, or until the sauce
just coats the back of a spoon. Check the seasoning.
Chop the fresh tarragon just before serving, sprinkle
over the chicken and serve with rice.

Chef's tip Make your own tarragon vinegar by placing a
sprig of fresh tarragon in a bottle of ordinary red or
white wine vinegar. After a week, strain out the tarragon
and your vinegar is ready. All your favorite herbs can be
used in this way.

Veal chops with Chablis en cocotte

A cocotte is a round or oval cooking pan with two handles and a tight-fitting lid that was traditionally used to cook slow-cooking dishes. Now "en cocotte" refers to braised dishes in which the meat is first browned and then cooked in a liquid at a low simmer either in the oven or on the stove top.

*Preparation time **15 minutes***
*Total cooking time **50 minutes***
Serves 4

4 veal loin chops, about 6 oz. each
1/4 cup unsalted butter
1/2 lb. veal trimmings or bones, finely chopped (ask the butcher)
1 cup Chablis wine
bouquet garni (see page 63)
3 oz. Canadian bacon, finely diced
1 small onion, finely chopped
1 carrot, finely diced
1 turnip, finely diced
1 tablespoon chopped fresh parsley

1 Season the veal chops with salt and pepper. In a large skillet over medium heat, melt two-thirds of the butter and brown the veal for 2–3 minutes on both sides. Once browned, transfer the chops to a plate. Add the trimmings to the pan and brown, then return the veal chops to the pan. Cover, reduce the heat and cook slowly for 4 minutes on each side. Transfer the chops and trimmings back to the plate and set aside. Increase the heat to medium-high and cook the meat juices, stirring constantly, for about 3–4 minutes, or until they have caramelized onto the bottom of the pan. Strain the trimmings to remove the excess fat and return to the pan. Add the Chablis and stir well, scraping the bottom, until the cooking juices have dissolved. Cook for about 5 minutes, or until the wine has reduced in volume by three-quarters. Add 2 cups water and the bouquet garni and simmer for 30 minutes. Strain the sauce into a glass measure and discard the veal trimmings and bouquet garni.

2 Meanwhile, melt the remaining butter in another skillet and brown the bacon for 2–3 minutes. Add the onion and carrot and cook for another 2 minutes before adding the turnip. Reduce the heat, cover and cook for 8 minutes.

3 Add the sauce to the vegetables, bring to a boil and cook for 10 minutes. Return the veal chops to the hot sauce, reduce the heat and allow to simmer for about 5 minutes, or until the veal is heated through. Serve immediately, sprinkled with the chopped parsley.

Braised lamb with tomato sauce

A simple yet delicious lamb stew, flavored with garlic, bacon and tomatoes, which can be served with rice or fresh pasta.

*Preparation time **25 minutes***
*Total cooking time **1 hour 45 minutes***
Serves 4

**2¹/₂ lb. boneless lamb shoulder, trimmed and cut into
  small pieces**
3 tablespoons oil
3 tablespoons unsalted butter
2 oz. Canadian bacon, diced
I small onion, chopped
I small carrot, chopped
2–3 tablespoons tomato paste
I tablespoon all-purpose flour
3 tomatoes, peeled, seeded and chopped
bouquet garni (see page 63)
4 cloves garlic, chopped
**2 cups brown stock (see page 63)
  or water**
I tablespoon chopped fresh parsley or basil

1 Preheat the oven to 350°F. Season the lamb with salt and pepper. Heat the oil in a heavy-bottomed skillet over medium-high heat, add the lamb and brown it, in batches, for about 6–8 minutes, or until well colored on all sides. Drain on paper towels.

2 Melt the butter in a large flameproof casserole or Dutch oven over medium heat. Add the bacon and cook until golden brown. Add the onion and carrot and cook for about 3 minutes. Stir in the tomato paste and cook for another 2 minutes. Sprinkle with the flour and bake for 5 minutes. Remove from the oven and mix in the flour. Add the tomatoes, bouquet garni and garlic. Place on the stove top and cook for 5 minutes, stirring constantly, then add the stock or water. Bring to a boil, stirring constantly. Add the lamb, cover and bake for 1 hour, or until the meat is tender when pierced.

3 Remove the meat from the sauce, cover and keep warm. Strain the sauce through a fine strainer, pressing well to extract as much liquid as possible. Discard the solids and pour the sauce into a saucepan.

4 Bring the sauce back to the boil, skimming if necessary. Simmer for 10 minutes, or until the sauce is thick enough to coat the back of a spoon. Add the lamb and stir until heated through. Season with salt and pepper. Sprinkle with the parsley or basil and serve.

Chef's techniques

◆

Disjointing a chicken

The flavor of a dish will often be better if, rather than buying pieces, you cut up a whole bird. This method of disjointing makes sure portions are evenly sized, and you can cut the chicken into four or eight pieces.

Use a pair of poultry shears to cut through the length of the breastbone.

Cut through the top third of the breast, leaving two equal portions. You can also remove the wing tips at this stage, if you wish.

Turn the chicken over and cut down either side of the backbone to completely remove it. The backbone should come away in one piece.

Separate the leg from the thigh by cutting through the leg joint.

Following the natural contours of the thigh, cut through to separate the breast and wing piece from the thigh and leg.

You now have eight chicken portions of equal size.

Repeat with the other half to produce four pieces.

Making chicken stock

*Good, flavorful homemade stock
can be the cornerstone of a great dish.*

Cut up 1 1/2 lb. chicken bones and carcass and put in a pan with a coarsely chopped onion, carrot and celery stalk. Add 6 peppercorns, a bouquet garni and 4 quarts water.

Bring to a boil and let the stock simmer gently for 2–3 hours, skimming off any foam that rises to the surface using a large spoon. Strain the stock through a strainer into a clean bowl, then allow to cool.

Chill the stock overnight, then lift off any fat. If you can't leave overnight, skim, then drag the surface of the hot strained stock with paper towels to lift off the fat. Makes 6–8 cups.

Making brown stock

*Roasting the bones gives a good color to the stock
and helps to remove the excess fat.*

In a 450°F oven, roast 3 lb. beef or veal bones for 40 minutes, adding a quartered onion, 2 chopped carrots, 1 chopped leek and 1 chopped celery stalk halfway through.

Transfer to a clean pan. Add 4 quarts water, 2 tablespoons tomato paste, bouquet garni and 6 peppercorns. Simmer for 3–4 hours, skimming often.

Ladle the stock in batches into a fine strainer over a bowl. Gently press the solids with the ladle to extract all the liquid and place in the refrigerator to cool. Lift off any fat. Makes 6–8 cups.

Freezing stock

*Stock will keep in the refrigerator for 3 days. It can
be frozen in portions for later use, for 6 months.*

After removing any fat, boil the stock until reduced to 2 cups. Cool and freeze until solid. Transfer to a plastic freezer bag and seal. To make 2 quarts stock, add 6 cups water to 2 cups concentrated stock.

Bouquet garni

*Add the flavor and aroma of herbs to your
dish with a freshly made bouquet garni.*

Wrap the green part of a leek loosely around a bay leaf, a sprig of thyme, some celery leaves and a few stalks of parsley, then tie with string. Leave a long tail to the string for easy removal.

First published in the United States in 1998 by Periplus Editions (HK) Ltd., with editorial offices at
153 Milk Street, Boston, Massachusetts 02109.

Murdoch Books and Le Cordon Bleu thank the 32 masterchefs of all the Le Cordon Bleu Schools, whose knowledge and
expertise have made this book possible, especially: Chef Cliche (MOF), Chef Terrien, Chef Boucheret, Chef Duchêne (MOF),
Chef Guillut, Chef Steneck, Paris; Chef Males, Chef Walsh, Chef Hardy, London; Chef Chantefort, Chef Bertin, Chef Jambert,
Chef Honda, Tokyo; Chef Salembien, Chef Boutin, Chef Harris, Sydney; Chef Lawes, Adelaide; Chef Guiet, Chef Denis, Ottawa.
Of the many students who helped the Chefs test each recipe, a special mention to graduates David Welch and Allen Wertheim.
A very special acknowledgment to Directors Susan Eckstein, Great Britain, and Kathy Shaw, Paris, who have been responsible for
the coordination of the Le Cordon Bleu team throughout this series.

The Publisher and Le Cordon Bleu also wish to thank Carole Sweetnam for her help with this series.

First published in Australia in 1998 by Murdoch Books®

Managing Editor: Kay Halsey
Series Concept, Design and Art Direction: Juliet Cohen
Editor: Elizabeth Cotton
Food Director: Jody Vassallo
Food Editors: Dimitra Stais, Tracy Rutherford
US Editor: Linda Venturoni Wilson
Designer: Michelle Cutler
Photographer: Jon Bader, Chris Jones
Food Stylist: Amanda Cooper, Mary Harris
Food Preparation: Tracy Rutherford, Kerrie Mullins
Chef's Techniques Photographer: Reg Morrison
Home Economists: Michelle Lawton, Kerrie Mullins, Kerrie Ray, Margot Smithyman

Library of Congress catalog card number: 98-85722
ISBN 962-593-447-2

Front cover: Paella

Distributed in the United States by
Charles E. Tuttle Co., Inc.
RR1 Box 231-5
North Clarendon, VT 05759
Tel: (802) 773-8930
Fax: (802) 773-6993

PRINTED IN SINGAPORE

05 04 03 02 01 00 99 98   10 9 8 7 6 5 4 3 2 1

Important: Some of the recipes in this book may include raw eggs, which can cause salmonella poisoning.
Those who might be at risk from this (the elderly, pregnant women, young children and those suffering
from immune deficiency diseases) should check with their physicians before eating raw eggs.